*In Folly's Shade*

ALSO BY JOHN WELCH

**Poetry**
*The Fish God Problem* (The Many Press, London 1977)
*And Ada Ann, A Book of Narratives*
                (Great Works Press, Bishops Stortford 1978)
*Out Walking* (Anvil, London 1984)
*Blood and Dreams* (Reality Street Editions, London 1991)
*Its Radiance* (Poetical Histories, Cambridge 1993)
*Greeting Want* (infernal methods, Cambridge 1997)
*The Eastern Boroughs* (Shearsman Books, Exeter 2004)
*On Orkney* (infernal methods, Stromness 2005)
*Collected Poems* (Shearsman Books, Exeter, 2008)
*Visiting Exile* (Shearsman Books, Exeter, 2009)
*Its Halting Measure* (Shearsman Books, Bristol, 2012)

**Prose**
*Dreaming Arrival* (Shearsman Books, Exeter, 2008)

**As editor**
*Stories from South Asia* (Oxford University Press, 1984)

# John Welch

# *In Folly's Shade*

Shearsman Books

First published in the United Kingdom in 2018 by
Shearsman Books
50 Westons Hill Drive
Emersons Green
BRISTOL
BS16 7DF

Shearsman Books Ltd Registered Office
30–31 St. James Place, Mangotsfield, Bristol BS16 9JB
*(this address not for correspondence)*

www.shearsman.com

ISBN 978-1-84861-619-6

Copyright © John Welch, 2018.
The right of John Welch to be identified as the author of
this work has been asserted by him in accordance with the
Copyrights, Designs and Patents Act of 1988.
All rights reserved.

ACKNOWLEDGEMENTS

Poems from this collection have appeared in the following print
and online magazines: *Active in Airtime, Ambit, Blackbox Manifold,
The Bow Wow Shop, Fire, Litter, Molly Bloom,
PN Review, Poetry London, Scintilla, Shearsman, Snow,
The Fortnightly Review, Tears In The Fence, Test Centre.*

Earlier versions of five of the six poems in 'Breeze's Counsel'
appeared in my collection *Its Halting Measure*
(Shearsman Books, 2012).

'Late' was published in
*The World Speaking Back: Poems for Denise Riley.*

# CONTENTS

## AT RANTERS LODGE

| | |
|---|---|
| Carpenter Build Me a House | 9 |
| A Provision | 10 |
| Translated | 13 |
| Antic Torso | 15 |
| Background Music | 16 |
| On the Hill | 17 |
| His Books | 19 |
| Jane | 20 |
| Having a Rest in 1953 | 21 |
| Out Walking: Wanstead Flats | 22 |
| Not at All | 23 |
| At Ranters Lodge | 29 |
| Breeze's Counsel | 34 |
| Out Walking: Walthamstow Marsh | 43 |

## IN FOLLY'S SHADE

| | |
|---|---|
| In Folly's Shade | 51 |
| A Blessing | 66 |
| Signing Off | 69 |
| At Culswick | 70 |

## INSIDE THE PANOPTICON

| | |
|---|---|
| Centre and Retreat | 77 |
| The Citizen Unharmed | 80 |
| Inside the Panopticon | 81 |
| Some Notes on Coinage | 85 |

## AN INTERZONE

| | |
|---|---|
| The Diarist | 91 |
| Pose | 92 |
| Late | 93 |
| Stone Boat | 94 |
| His Night Thoughts | 95 |
| The Paradise File | 98 |
| Taken Flight | 101 |
| Squandered Glances | 104 |
| | |
| Notes | 107 |

One

AT RANTERS LODGE

## CARPENTER BUILD ME A HOUSE

*His poetic spirit still shows itself to be active. For instance in my house he saw the drawing of a temple. He told me to make one out of wood. I replied that I have to work for my living, that I am not fortunate enough to live in philosophic calm like him.*
Zimmer, on the poet Hölderlin

As if in translation eating the bread of existence
In here is a creaking voice, turning the handle
And it does so happen sometimes just before sleep
With that slight awkwardness of language
When it takes you to another voice
As if inhabiting a seizure.

Finding the lines the poet
Wrote, in the shadow of form
Is it all done in imitation?
Among the wreckage,
Who lead such careful lives –
Each step I take
But there has to be some purchase
And it's still as if that music
Were issuing out of
Someone else's side.

Loftily all the same
We'll carry it forward.

# A PROVISION

*To provide air for human breath*
        Kafka

What was it they were doing? Seen from a distance it looked as though it could be work. They went about it as if it were something they were beholden to. It was by and large a solitary occupation though with outbursts of uneasy sociability.

It was not his idea, this language, but waking at night he felt huge making words. Next day when he looked at them it was like lifting a mirror to flight. Do we want our signs *in order to* set them free?

'Way Out To All Exits Lift Stairs And Fiction'. Yes and look at him standing out there in all weathers, saying 'It is the thing that nearly makes me live.'

Upstart lyric impulse and, next to her skin, the paltriness of language, which is why he has come here dressed in these heavy clothes.


Sitting in an upstairs room he is trying to arrive somewhere, making his own silence on behalf of something he can almost remember. In those odd corners of being where still he waits for himself, a fountain playing in a desert. He watches the water fade, dissembling, into the ground.

'The words', he said 'were to gain me a purchase on it, their empty grip on the page like a bird's claws' – and how neat the whole thing's workings, like the insides of an old-fashioned watch.

This self, an emptiness he can return to after the clutter of words while downstairs there's a silence whose edge frays with voices.

Getting tired of the game it is playing you can see these 'works' one by one lifted heavily into the air. Watched through a window everything he knows is there tied in a loose bundle.

'Which part of me do you want to search today?'

The distress was real enough even as he watched its performance. A 'performance' – that is, he means what he does and slowly you can see him become what he is.

A careful staging of the self, he'd made up this continuous voice. All this for the lack of a hearer?

The tempter: 'You are nearer to it than most'.

The paper was an invitation, its creamy folds, saying 'There is plenty more for you'.

'The book I take with me' he says 'is everywhere unread'.


His subdued venom. Giving himself away like an empty token. 'It was another life, the one I had.' But these people – artists? – leading such interestingly selfish lives.

Over to here is where it now comes, nearer by far, a language, something that empties itself full. In the end there are only the words to smooth the thing.

Reading the poems and briefly noting their passing, each was a nod of acknowledgement – as if staving something off? Light-proofed the darkness in his mind, its indigent posture. Writing it out was stepping carefully round something, or someone, lying in the road. The fascination of a self-contained world of images, its dusty glitter, where words 'blaze'. It was a moody adolescent's place of safety, a peculiar talent pacing corridors carpeted with rain. Somewhere outside the air freshened.

Empty blessing of moonlight, someone still holding out just under the surface.

When the path ran away with itself he tried to follow.

In due course it would declare its own downfall.

Like a wordless book opening under the sky, a fish dying with the sky in its mouth.

Yes, to be small again, and inside the window's stare

This Orpheus, in mourning he must cradle his own head.

## TRANSLATED

An exile: being floated across such impossible borders
he'd arrived here – the silent weight of a door that opened
just enough, so that now he looks out over our rooftops,
waking each day to their outline as if to an illness. I think
of him waking in there in the afternoon still trapped in
his dream of arrival. Splashing water over his face, perhaps
he notices the way the sunlight enters, how it catches on a
tap's metal with such bright authority.

I'd helped him make this translation and now it hovers
between us like an anxious shade. Facing all ways at once,
an unmarked milestone, he's the figure behind me as I get
up to leave. I find I can hardly get out of his door. I carry
its shadowy architrave like an overcoat as I move away
carefully and out into the beleaguered crowd. It's as if
trying to borrow his exile I might make myself lonely, a self
imperfectly remembered.

Being thus translated he is a man with his words stranded
halfway over a bridge. Came to a nation gloomy with
the aftermath of empire – and one day he might come
to know it, his otherness elided in those voices? 'Yes this
is someone's home. No harm in anyone that's here.' In
the meantime, back in there those desk-silences. Outside,
the walls are covered in layers of writing. It's tagging, not
political slogans, here in this depleted city where shadows
sometimes attain a short substance, smashing and stealing.

And the rest of *my* life – as if I were reading not very
adequate translation? Seeing round the words I think I
can just make out the original where it busies itself with
cooking, sorting papers, arranging flowers. As I watch one
opens like the remains of an eye.

Out walking on the Heath here's a tree that harbours a wound. It glistens and dries where I stand and look out over London. Here are the words that almost found me, I imagine how they might all come down in one enormous descending, as the cracked tree's lightning-self once held to that split in the light. Yoked together the two of us, filling the wound with sound.

# ANTIC TORSO

*Christopher Middleton's 'Anasphère: le torse antique' (1978)*

Borrowed
      Axe was swung
           Spatter of blood in the air

The way the words take flight –
Such lightness belongs in language

A refusal it
Finds, in me somewhere

Since all the rest
Is only what I remember

And someone keeps making these books.

There remained an idea of sea
Each bird an idea of sky

To come at it fresh again
The voice as if it came
In search of me

Other people's words
That send me back to it

A simple lake
      Its waterfowl
           A resolve
As near as words can get
There to take shelter
As of someone or something bounding along
The way their movement emptied the dance.

# BACKGROUND MUSIC
*i.m. Christopher Middleton*

I woke up not knowing quite where I was
Here in this hotel by the sea
Guests feeding, breakfasts of shamed meat
A mud of coffee. Picking the remnants
Out of my teeth against the faint background music
But what will become of us,
All those half-used soaps, shampoos?
We have 'needs', they have remedies
And all the small noises they make round the edge of us
Footfall-quiet as if respecting a corpse
In this hospital of particulars
With staff and guests helping each other along.
'It's where I sometimes go to write poems'
I hear myself starting to say –
But all the time there's the faint, infernal music.
This ash of sound, it will settle us to oblivion
And before that one final meal, each fragment
Held in the mouth till it perish? Outside
The clouds are still a procession going nowhere
And I am lying here being beholden to silence.
Lest I become desultory
I think of the things I am trying to make.
But next day at breakfast reading your words
How oddly fresh they'll sound.

## ON THE HILL

Forests, on the edge of cities –
Going out on an expedition,
And finding a smashed bird in the road

A small space opens
Under a pigeon's
Insistent afternoon call.

Out on the hill my life's
A remote preaching of sunlight –
I can see it, almost, from here.

Dry shapes of words that rub together
Can make a dusty light
A frail thing, distant from blood,

But to hang about here
In the hawthorn's musky smell?
We climbed out onto the hill

Letting eye starve
On a hill slope where the animals
Tug and nuzzle perpetually

The many-angled stones
So close-set in their wall
They appear to be in flight.

A wind came rushing down
Through the slope's sessile oaks.
In a dull panic I was alone,

And asked 'What will spill out of us,
This chaos, mine and yours?'
Was this the trick, to throw the mind away?

Seen from there the sea was quiet as milk.
Together we walked to the shore
Then home, through several miles of English rain.

It was an act of faith
Leaving the words in those void arms
To come home in the storm.

If I could show you. If I could show,
Being here like the water's continual
Murmur against a door of sunlight –

It was always about to come alive.
The language was a kind of devouring.
And then the tedium of the finished thing.

## HIS BOOKS

When the poet died
What happened to his collection of books?
There were four or five shelves of poetry.
The dealer who came took only a few
The collectable ones with signatures, greetings.
Now the poet's widow is baffled.
She surveys them spread out all over the floor.
'I don't want the shelves
Completely bare' she had said
'But look, there are far too many'.
I imagine the poet's final moments. He's thinking
'Why is there suddenly all this space inside me?'
As he finds himself slipping away
Sideways then up, high into the air.
Perhaps he looked back down
And saw the books still safe in their shelves
And then they were trying to rise up
On only one wing, to join him
But being held back by the substance of paper
Here they are now, all over the floor
In their awkward, toppling piles.

## JANE

Listen to it, the sound of grief
Where she lies in the cage of her cot
Sunlight striking the curtain,
Parents still playing outside.
On the way to where
The sun is ending its journey
The child will eventually finish her crying,
Settle to sleep, our words
One day finding their way to her mouth.
This keeping self together,
It's a cradle slung in the air.
But the tongue, like a wagging finger,
Admonishes 'This is what there is'.
Is this a rehearsal? Still hearing
Those quietened voices that come
From further off now, and each time
Learning to sleep again.

## HAVING A REST IN 1953

Every day after lunch we had to have a 'rest',
A half hour or so. In silence we lay on our beds
Each with its red top blanket. We were supposed to read.
It's the books of escape I remember
From the Second World War, *The Wooden Horse,*
*The Great Escape*, *The Colditz Story*.
Sometimes Ramsden and I would play 'dot cricket'.
The phantom paper runs piled up.
But thinking about it now there was
A paradoxical sense of freedom
Being not yet part of the world.
It went with that peculiar sense of estrangement,
Banished to an eighteenth century house
At the end of a long drive. At the end of each term
Caught between here and there
I'd come back home, and find myself the stranger.
Now I can see myself
On that station platform again
And all those boys, twenty or so to a room
Reading, or just pretending
Each lying on his red blanket
In a fidgety silence, each with his square of sky.

# OUT WALKING: WANSTEAD FLATS

A temple around here somewhere
The map forewarns, a golf course
And City of London Cemetery.
On the way from the station you passed
Seven Poles talking, under a tree
Still just in full leaf.
Maybe you don't arrive at a country,
A country arrives at you.
Looking for somewhere to die
Someone might set off into a city,
Its omens flashing on screens, shakily
But walking like this you are being detached
From two separate places
And, waist-high in grass now,
Standing out here the world seems flat.
Moving across it you seem to attract
The city's roar, then its murmur.
Leaving that residue of sound
Like this you can walk yourself into
A particular sort of silence. Returning
And crossing, at the chicane, yours is
A trajectory hard to plot.
You do imagine the cameras
Even here, suspended from trees perhaps?
Back on the station platform, six minutes to go.
The last flowers open their mouths, and
'For god's sake man just chill' –
She's talking to the puppy
While a paper dart's erratic progress
On the platform opposite
Is the wind in its performance
Catching it like that, a baffler.
'Mine died' the child says, watching it
As it flutters down onto the track.

## NOT AT ALL

*Hero*

*The head of hair* theft of a flame
At the extreme west of desire
To unfold the whole
Is placed *I was going to say*
*A diadem died*
On the crowned brow where it was first of all lit.

A naked tender hero defames
The woman who

But without gold to sigh
That this vivid nude
The fire always lit from within
Originally the only one continues
In the eye's jewel, truthful or mocking.

*Lute*

'Go break this lute upon the coach's wheel'
Whose fragments are so much more
And darkness to the left of the word.

'The red-leaved table of my heart' –
A comic strip quality
The anatomical aspect
Pressed into a ridiculous figure.

'While others are eating of oysters I'm writing.
Kiss my cuff
I never breathe but I think of you'.

Their gestures comment on the action
The lute like a woman's body
A horrible image of torture
Transformed into an exquisite conceit.

'Broken on the wheel is my last music'


*City of Light*

The immigrant serving breakfast at the hotel
Is caught in a shaft of sunlight
Whose horse is more than human,
A memory of fading trees
When, though a torn gate of paper
A valley of sky!

*The friends of purgatory*
*Please respect the silence.*
*This is a church*
*You can visit with your telephone.*

They heaped up buildings against the sky
*F[r]iction    one soul*
*Courtyard of the green oak*
*The daughters of Calvary*
Passages of a lost music.

*Lets observe life in protected spaces*
Beginning up there in the trees.

But Papa what was it built for?

*Manifest*

Appeal to 10.000 young students who signed the declaration about the West, April 1920: UNOVIS MANIFESTO 'We Want' furnishing much of Vitebsk in Suprematist art and propaganda.

He designed architectons, model buildings without a specified purpose or setting.

White forms against a white background, a final liberation from the world of visible forms: 'Painting died, like the old regime, because it was an organic part of it.'

Meanwhile, the black square as a collective signature, we saw him go. Abruptly he shouldered his way through the crowd.


*Found in an Album*

Holly, persistent
Its bright berries
To withstand city air, sea winds.

The weeping pendula,
A female berry-bearing form
Which makes a low bower.

Many with pale cream margins
Nearly white-edged leaves
On a weeping, domed crown.

But broadly elliptic leaves
Have a metallic, greyish sheen.
From a distance

Marbled several shades
Of green to a dark margin
It lightens a dark corner.


*Whose Lyric Utterance*

'The enthusiastic audience listened carefully to the reading of informal letters from unknown people and then destroyed a huge symbolic writing-case.

Keeping wings next to himself
And how many ounces of flight is the bird?
It was another life, the one he had.
Finding he can't believe in it after all
He goes back to bed, her quiet breathing beside him.
Yes, couples do take refuge in one another
And it might be a kind of relief when, setting it down at last
He can just catch the sound of it, as it collapses,
That whole remote apparatus.


*The Way Ahead?*

First of all, establish an archive.
Raising the structure, abandoning it
He waits for the meaning to seep in
The firm impress of his prose,
A scurrying in the bushes.

The avant-garde's a backward look.
It almost sounds like a translation
Being *carried across* like this,
To where exactly?

Carefully distressed, its façade's
A comfortable place to be behind,
Each poem like a small request.


*The Bravado*

A bravado of sky
& the words, how they carry themselves.
I'll do your waiting for you.
For that I have been granted an extra name.

The cringing process I travel to be near –
'Why haven't we heard of this man?'
No it wasn't the sound of somebody falling.
Someone looks into the matter.

While an aeroplane lifts its head.
Slowly over the town, the bridges bow
Or bow. As I'm carried off
I never had a style, or even a 'true voice'.

When I looked all around me
Perhaps I *was* the panopticon.
The mirror stops me seeing, without it
I am an emptiness at the centre.

I'm someone running away from his heartland.
Exhausted but still awake.
Keeping one step ahead of revelation
I really should write a book about it,

All that richness, as you approach
That potential. But as you get closer
The language seems to evaporate
Like a sweat of desire. It goes to a shimmer

Like writing on a coin's shallow glare.
But it gives me a leg to stand on.
Here they come on their hobbled feet
Waving broken hands.

Looking back at the dream I am in it.
My body is only a memory now
Still seeking forgiveness –
To possess is to be possessed

When looking all round me I found
I had gained another head.
It was a lonely seizure
An awkward consecration.

## AT RANTERS LODGE

*He took his bath with unalloyed satisfaction between four bare walls, whereon certain dimly-curtained squares in the extended whiteness indicated the exile of all art except that of the air, the sun and the wind… 'I mean that it's like the way you feel about things' she explained, 'when you hear the rain outside, while reading a book. You know what I mean. Oh I can't put it into words…' I know just what you mean' he said.*
John Cowper Powys, *Wolf Solent*

No, it's not Conjuror's Lodge
And I'm not a Primitive Methodist
But here at the start of an almost-island
Opposite The Dead House
And knowing the waves aren't traffic
We'll sleep better.

It's an odd sort of house, where we sleep
On a platform right at the top.
Taking myself to bed
There's something perfect inside me
I cannot ever quite reach –
If it could only settle on a title.

Going out walking was a way of finding
If the words might shine back into you.
I imagined it might come together
Casually, like flowers propped in a vase
But, ornamental dust, these evocations
Stay sealed in an airtight jar

Lying here now on what she calls the day bed
Reading steadily, sheltered from the rain
It is a satisfying room,
But the 'exile of all art'

Known by the marks
Their frames have left behind?

While the house fills up, with stones the guests have chosen.

*At Weymouth*

The sea's
        just *there* –
It's Weymouth in the mist.

The resort dwindles.
Is this a listening post?
Turn back. Thirty six pedalos
Are drawn up in ranks
And every one has its own name.

Steady rain    the verbal fuss.

*Inland*

We had come to the good place,
A coastline rich with fossils,
The animals' dried dung
Being blown across the hillside.
Like two men who'd met in a dream
Our talk was eating the air
And somewhere over to the left
The unreachable sea. Thrift, speedwell, eyebright
Yes, flowers with names like that.
The sea that day was breathing-still. 'Can't you see,
It's about trying to win something back'

. . .

The countryside was anxious notices.
No one's to be seen at work in the fields.

As we tread our way into it
With an awkward reverence

Crossing a fast-flowing stream,
Its unimpeachable water,

A hillside of slow cattle
Devoutly feeding

A field of long grass
Silvered in the wind, a sheet fast-flowing,

And, somewhere over there,
A fake giant with an enormous erection.

*Chesil Bank*

*Die Sprache spricht* and *vouloir dire* –
Everywhere it speaks it wants to say,
Those times I stayed up half the night
Trying to find its singing in my head
Like tinnitus. Out here

Tamarisk lies stretched out over stones.
Some plants there are can colonise this shingle –
Campion, sea-kale
As if they had just landed there.
It's hard to see how they take root

And Babbington's Leek, like a shy
But irrepressible stranger
Is moving onto the shingle's edge.

Over the other side is all that water.
We're staying on the landward side.

I try to be more or less contained
In what it is I have to say
Straining against the wind,
When over there I see a man
Way out on the enormous bank of stones.

He's on his own, appropriating distance.
Fishing, or just standing there
He's starting to mean
Maybe because there's only one of him
Whose mind goes, stretched out, over all that water

As if to celebrate each helpless encounter
With still more words.
Perhaps it is the sea has too much voice.
Outdistancing his code
It has a gift for appropriating silence.


*Fortune's Well*

*Fortuneswell . . . The only place on Portland with a pretty name but the town itself is of a plangent self-assertive devil-may-care ugliness. Some giant, when it was building, must have thrown a few handfuls of dry cement on it, and nobody since has swept them up . . . a pretty cottage in Portland would be like lipstick on a fishwife.*
         Aubrey de Selincourt, in the series 'Visions of England'.

Lipstick on a fishwife, what lips wish?
At 8am going to buy scallops
The fisherman asked 'You want shell or meat?'
But something falling was a sound I heard,
Vocabulary that shifted in a storm?
This 'island' after all

Was one enormous quarry.
At our approach each prison makes
Its special silence all around
And we sit in our tent of phrases
To ponder the 'vision of England'.
What you watch, it is watching you here,
Abandoned installations everywhere,
The constant wind's dispersals,
Its way of making
Gardens among these rocks –
It blows a fine dust over everything,
But, in each careful pause for breath,
Warm scribe, these stones
Are almost all of it
And far too much to carry home.


*Coda*

The Visitors' Book:
Temporary occupation
Endlessly supplied

Terminate these applications

# BREEZE'S COUNSEL

*Cheshunt to Broxbourne and back.*

Walking steadily
Like this, beside the water
Does bring a certain kind of peace.
Discarded blossom lies along the surface,
All this stuff that's drifting down
And a powerful scent of elder
Whose musk is edged with sweetness.
People you pass are not quite sure
Whether or not to greet you
And here's a sort of bollard
It's like an abandoned phallus.

Trees have that hint of greyness,
Just before coming into full leaf
Against a dark threat of sky.
You carry on, through surprising groves
Putting some distance under your feet
Till, breaking into the open
Space of a silent field, there are
Unmoving clouds
And what's this shrub with whitish flowers,
Its musty-spermy smell? And so
You turned back to that waterside
Whose floating cargo of blossom
Was almost as motionless as text.

*Deal to Dover*

'The cloud-heart melts away' —Lord de Tabley

The surprise of nothing being found
the pupil shrinks in so much light
and our restlessness, against
an odd still sea
its peculiar deeps and blues –

Danger Of Death
No Diving
No Jumping
      the sea's
steep syllables.

Mid-afternoon, yes
but why should words help.
What is beyond
this beckoning?
        It had
  fixed itself
  like a brooch
  but awkwardly, at my side.

When the reader gets up from the book
it is as if he is almost in paradise
and still that expanse before him
imagining it an audience
and it saying 'I want every inch of you'
but he has no name to find it with

and how the night becomes us
when you'll fit me like a glove,
you and I
meticulous graveyard of speech.

*In the Sensory Garden, Hunstanton*

Marsh Hawkshead, Rough Clover
Many-spiked Goosefoot, Seaside Catchfly –
They are names you can't quite believe in.
A couple of hundred yards inland
Just underneath each name
The plants' outlines are sculpted
On slabs, like gravestones
Arranged in a semi-circle.
The names are in Braille as well, raised dots
On small strips of metal glued down.
You think of a hand that brushes against
The almost-substance of words
Then turn, and look down the slope.
In the middle-distance is some kind of fir tree
Leaning slightly – it looks like a character
As it bows to the water beyond it
And all the sea's names.

*Ash Cloud, Kew Gardens*

The language was an accident
That happened somewhere in the creature's brain
And somewhere like a window swinging open, somewhere's
A landscape with its mouthings of trees.
There are the words that will not need you
Collecting in silence all around your mouth,
A careful heap of fallen petals. All the same
They make it sound as if you almost meant it
Distracted from 'self', set free to rhapsodize.
You think it really ought to last for ever.

Somewhere inside this amiable jungle
There waits a label not designed to be read –
*A jay can bury five thousand acorns in autumn..*
*Can you afford the planet?*
Here at the edge of what we almost know
It flowers, as if in hiding
The words hung out in rows like changeless blossom
Against a sky whose blue
Once made us intensely happy
But noticed most when gone, our words
Arranged like scented gardens for the blind.

*Whose Breaths*

Outside on the grass and densely scattered
The pear-blossom. Getting walked inside the house
It makes a sort of reverse pilgrimage.

And the clean living smell,
It's a sense of her in the mind,
The petals underfoot so much crushed detail.

What the words conceal is what we are moving towards.
I'll try to disturb the surface of things
As little as possible.

The absence that there is in me
Was what I found to celebrate
A fresh quiet smell. Shallow epiphany.

The burden was somewhere in front of me
Shone, lazily. Stepping out
Into a hidden romance of storms

To have found it again intact,
The thoughtful container,
Its shifting stain of consciousness

On the lip of its creatureliness,
To live without consolation?
The poem ending it happens again and again

Like hearing from somewhere far off the sound of land,
And we imagine returning
The things to their proper names

The plainness of our speech being fed to earth.

*At Hollow Ponds, Epping Forest*

*Where the chimpanzee is able to recognise that the mirror is an epistemological void, and to turn his attention elsewhere, the child has a perverse will to remain deluded.*
                    Lacan

1
A cold grey day in early March.
Travelling with a swarm of them
We're two of the conspirators
While these implacably cheerful children
Cross the bald ground. In the bushes
The five year old finds a dead fox:
'It smells like rotten fish'.

Hanging back, watching, hearing their voices
Arrive as if from nowhere,
And travelling over the threadbare carpet of sound
I wasn't sure I was still there beside you.
Flying apart we flew along together
Each caught in the same storm.
Much later we'll return to the grove.


2
A reflection thin as the sheet of paper
On which I am writing this now,
A flood of ink like a shadow retreating inwards.
And a child who struggled to express this gift –
Do you falter? The mirror is tall.
Why do you follow what turns you away?
Seeing yourself in a mirror
You are looking at silence, beside you
The patience of a waiting name.

3
As if this were an aberration,
These clicks in the silence – the language
It is within us scheming
Something bolted on
To a cautious lyric gift,
These sounds an aspiration,
Our little puffs of air. Look down
And see where below us
It opens a splendid page.
I shall lower my self
Cautiously into that silence

But the hopefulness a child might feel
At the start of a new day.
As the animals stirred one by one
They greeted him with their eyes.
Wings half-hidden behind him
Enchanted by the trap does he find
There is freedom in falling to earth,
To land in a stumbling world?
Do you falter? Tell me you falter.

*Breeze's Counsel*

*They forget the dust for a little music*
                       Roland Penrose

Glad to be there
Not any longer, but now
This interval, of
        walking
Back to it, over the leaves –
A breeze blows the shadows about
As if we were inside it
Like a slightly disordered mind.


What language blinks at
As light as hunger
Gets covered with a cloth of sound.

Like watching birds – it's always
Just over there the
Startled life in it

Some significant birdsong
And I only write it all down to defend myself
From all that noise.


Given almost enough with which to dissemble
The words, like someone shamming dead
Whose words battled the stillness
Or like the names of stations rushing past

Till calmed by snow this silent other
Is lifted onto the arms of trees.

White perfume cooled to zero
What might be spilt becomes an effect of silence,
The future sealed for a time
And later to see it slipping away,
A tainted, patchwork effect
The unheard sound as epitaph.


The brush-and-ink poets
Are tracing their names

Halting lyric     a nagging wish
'He Carries His Instrument Home'

What I dismembered
Yes take it home, splash it with wine

In a city. Whose poor are pushed to its rim
Cheap orchids     breeze's counsel.

## OUT WALKING: WALTHAMSTOW MARSH

And so dis-
   cover late
Energies, rising   and here it
Comes,
        That voice again –
Yes, and seventy years of voice
What's to show for it?
                All too often
It was like diving into
An insignificant lake.

Going out   first thing
The flatness of streets
Alert for any sign

Another day of
Graffiti's trapped energies,
And yes, all these bodies
Every one has its flaw.

'Calorie restriction
To enhance life expectancy'
A pill   to relieve pressure.
Take one, in the morning
You have nothing to lose
But what remains of your life

It's the sum of its parts.
But pulling in different directions
It came to pieces in my hands!

*From Wilsons Hill*

*Wilsons Hill. The hillside is unique in Hackney and this region because of its ecology and geology status. It has a mixture of spring ares (sic) with Thistles and Willowherd (sic). For further information phone…*

There is no one there. So leave your message –
Misspelling equals illumination?
'Have your say on dog control in Hackney'
Let go your inner wolf.

My head is full of flight,
A thistle, its head full of seed.
Echolaliac, hearing voices
There are noises everywhere on my island
As well as this singing inside my right ear.

Relentless epiphanies   clinical measures . . .
The words might *dissolve* this noise in my head?

Hunched like that, learning bodily grief
Ekstasis   it was
A 'standing outside', and when I came back
The words were waiting, it was as if they mourned
That absence, a brief loss of self

Hearing the runners their tap tap tap
One by one, behind me.
Lee Valley Ice Rink
National Cycle Network.
'We think your poem suffers
Significance overload
But welcome to Walthamstow Nature Reserve'

Six cattle released here to graze
As if to redeem pastoral.

'Trees of Interest in Springfield Park'
Yes the place has anxious guardians.
'I often come down here first thing
To meditate briefly'.

Canary Wharf in haze, three miles distant.
                              On a picnic table
There are five empty cans   like temple offerings
The dew still on them,

Is that linaria?
'An Italian introduction escaped from our gardens
Has taken to the UK like a native
Grows out of walls, and the cracks in concrete'.
This city's a concrete mulch

Meanwhile, the convenience of this breeze
In the way it turns those rows of leaves
Upward to an attractive paleness
Like watching the underside of a language

And here's an abandonment of wild roses.
Adolescent elder, brambles
Picturesque at the base of the pylon.
The sky's a sudden tinge of blue,
The heat for a moment unshielded. It goes again
This voice not quite your voice, cuts in and out.
Being spoken for I turn back
Mindful of this enjoyment.

Turning back to the river
A plastic bag blows along behind me
Dogging my heels,
Floating islands of vegetation
Houseboat owners emerging
Sleepily from their craft.

Three canada geese, passing low overhead
In copious flight
                    Creak of their wings
The particular sound of two swans in flight
Thin steady beat of the air in their pinions
Keeping me company.

Seen from the bank that large patch of light on the water,
Mobile effect of the sunlight
That's caught on the ripples so that it seems to be getting
Closer and closer as if to engulf me.
But, using that branch in front of it as a marker,
It's just an illusion.


Back up the hill, picking up voices,
It's Sabbath  the Hassid
Is coming towards me.
Does he ever ask himself
'Why am I wearing all these clothes?'

It being the Sabbath that day she'd asked me in
To turn her heating down. Inside
We found shelf upon shelf of the law
Trapped in a glass-fronted bookcase

People who live by the book. Someone said
'They have words for only two kinds of flower
Violet and rose'.
                    Passing the Moslem Girls School
'Smile you're on CCTV'

Inscriptions in Arabic, Hebrew.
People are edging together in cities,
Like a lake's rising waters.

They'll emerge from domestic palaces
Sitting out on the steps, the beautiful ones
Man woman and child   taking the city air
There is music somewhere behind them

Stepping out to an undiscovered rhythm
As if in a stately dream
They were coming towards us their heads held high –
Remember when we all sat down together
Politely edging closer?

Reach through a fence of words
Striding on heedfully.


*The Voice*

Talk of a beautiful sameness everywhere
I'm edging towards. But pulled up short
There is always the slight sense
Of seeing yourself in a mirror.

In a frenzy of impotence scraps of verse
Are occasional gleams in the shallows.
There's the fascination of the thing itself
And a war against enchantment.

The aim of it – is it almost us?
But the target is blind, its cyclops eye
And the language swarm in the head –
This surplus is what divides me

And yes, this voice. I'd imagined it
There in all my speech.
With that odd faith it had in itself
I might walk it all over London.

Down here, in a couplet-neat silence
And seeking to establish
A last connection I stride
Heedfully on past the nondescript,

Words inscribed on the inside of a tomb
That's sealed with a curse,
And what dust improvises
Is thrown up into the air

Breath-taking   a text
Leans into the wind
As a page comes out whole
Turning lazily on the sky.

# Two

## IN FOLLY'S SHADE

# IN FOLLY'S SHADE

*How shall she know my griefs? I'll drop the paper.*
 *Sweet leaves, shade folly…*
                        Love's Labours Lost

*Prelude*

Palaeolithic? To use
Being to eat in that language
As it moved through the world
Ingested the sky, and
This one? He brought forth demons
Dreaming
In his plume of night air
What he wanted – mostly the language,
An untiring mirror.

…

'I made it in the void of you
Burrowing into the temple'.

So saying I lifted the mirror
Up to myself
As, near to impossible tears
I remembered an absolute purity of flight

Turned back into myself one final time:
Like being inside the process of a flower.

…

Not you exactly but
A space transfigured.
Desire gave something to survive for.

'Not just a question' I think
'Of breathing life into –
Do I have to take *her* into *me*?'
This figure of liveliness
That I watch and I hunger for. Yes
There were two of us so we fled to that meal.

...

At twilight, as grass advances
Towards the darkening threshold
High above me
The swifts are eating the air.

She is a richness of promise even now
Our alliance of hunger
While the moving dots, birds in the distance
Stand clear to compose an image.

I

Infant bone and blood
Genesis moves forward

Birth packet
Something that comes from inside
Streaked stone   bundle of lightnings
When helpless and gentle it entered the day.

...

Suffolk winter garden
Desire mouthing around,
Love-tangle in a wood.
The undersides of mirrors

Infant feelings,
Reflected here they move like weather
Across the page of the face.

Rasp of light a winter knowledge
Light's unholy delight
The battle is early
The food is inside itself
Infant yell in a muddle of air.
A flight of steps has settled
Just here, like a flock of birds.

...

Eating what is outside itself
Being what it mainly does
It incorporates the gloss of sunlight.
Something like a mirror stands over the bed.
It has dozens of little feet and walks on its hands
Gets up into it, climbing a ladder of air.

It was as if something had climbed inside him
And speech makes them glad, the language harness,
Its sentence
        Is ushered into being
To incorporate the silent other.

...

Out in the garden early
Window catching the light –
Flight of a headless bird.
This epiphany of flight
It's like an extra sense of smell.

...

I wakened my breath
An exile bloomed on the mirror.
In a stone church looking out
From the one available window
On the edge of a plain shaft of light
I'm looking out over the field,
No skull here   nor redeemer
Only the earth-damp smell
Faint blooms of lichen
Where stone and earth make a perfect join.
Yes I'm here, and in here
What I contain, it contains me,
Seed   tissue   web   and rain.


2


On a cold November morning
I wait on a station platform

Above ground now and somewhere in North London
Not far from the place I was born

And I think I am coming home.
Breath hangs in the air, an estrangement

As of sense from its owner? A draught of sensation
As the train pulls in is something unnameable.

The train slides open its doors
And I feel I'll step off into nowhere.

The topmost part of a tree
Still glows in the sun.

For the time being I'm suspended here
Where something ends and nothing begins.

…

Day after day I'd watch as the sky
Went brighter behind their houses
Just before the day ended

And the face of hurt turned inward.
I was held in that loose knot.

'Give me the animal-human
And turn your face to me, my friend'.

…

Albion – arrived on the island
Almost all in one piece

It being about this time
That I'd entered into my power

Whose childhood now hears its bird
Elusive again in the elm.

What light takes away it gives back
That special post-coital sheen on the leaves.

Walking back furiously
I feel emptied by all this sun.

A gap in thought
Birds flying off into twilight

No there is no one at all in there
This is the emptiest interview

And what 'meaning' implies –
The loss of all that potential?

…

There were stories being told
To bind up wounds

Print columns steadily inching
Into the sky. Down here

Under bare branches
I could watch the light thicken.

But just before this
Yes, it seemed to grow more clear

In a silence whose lengthening arm
Extended into the void.

…

Each branch in the suburb
Hung out its drops of recent rain.

In such bright damp a bird
Will sing away like mad,
An entertainment

And in the small place left
I'd lift my eyes and turn,
Live being surrounded
By carefully selected unread books,

All that nourishment
That I'm in sight of
             And then
My foot being set
Onto one possible new step
Before the evening
Arrived with its levelling darkness
To sit in the breath.

...

Being made love to by an enormous absence
Alone in the room with a mirror
Thought hard of something, lets say a woman,
What thought goes hard inside
Her neatly folded there-ness.
The politics of the gaze grows wistful.

...

The wound has all the appearance of silence.
Where its scar grows
This 'I' might be a replacement.
As if to outwit solitude
Writing its own memorial
It wiped its mouth, looked round
Then returned to a hesitant murmur of itself.

...

December, reeds
Round the back of
Industrial dereliction

Sky beaten down into water
That trails the reflection of clouds

Explosions of bird-life, each one
Is the quick bead of an eye
And voices that speak from below

As if I were someone quite else.
A machine, fed toner ash
Was quietly humming under a window –

The glass-denatured light
This was a well-made silence.


3  *After Du Bellay*

I saw a fountain coming from dumb rock
Bright as crystal in the rays of sun.
Lovely sand was yellow under there.

Nature worked with art
To bring together in one place
All the pleasures of the eye.

Breeze heard itself
Singing itself to sleep
And you were somewhere in it.

Seats, ranged beside the water
Were white as bodies.
A hundred nymphs had gathered there

When down from the nearby mountain
A pack of fauns descended yelling,
With filthy dabble troubled the quiet wave

And put those nymphs to flight.

…

I carried you in me in case
The mirror should swallow me whole

Now I'll approach the page
That all those creatures ran from

And in the jostling press
Of bodies that fly from me

My fearful self's in hiding
My fearful self the follower.

Headless I advance
A disembodied singing.

But the loving gaze is other
And still will not come home to me.

Stretched verse is a membrane
Is what I can make from my hunger.

…

To wait out my hope
Was my good fortune.

Reclaim the image in the mirror –
I am what flies from my grasp

So take out the axe that's buried in silence
And walk off into the desert

But such an expanse of flesh?
How workmanlike is desire

Still, it possesses strangeness.

4

To join
      m'othering,
Firstborn, what I feel full of.

A fact in the world
I was born, sister
Later at my side.

Round behind me was
Me everywhere
I caught myself hiding behind the door.

...

Kouros nuzzled by the light
His angled planes of stone
Always moving forward
To where a small warrior
Gathers his immense shield.

...

Our parents are the king and queen
There's no way round it –
We've buried them in photographs.

We bury them in light
We bury them to keep them
And come, how like a startled bride, to language.

All this was written to the sleeping child.

...

My feeling of bafflement
When I saw my daughter's 'family'
A small figure of each of us
She had made, and I was convinced
There was one too many.
I could not make out who was who for a moment
Then I stood there in front of it
For quite some time.


5

Daybreak, one feather's
Enough to lift the sky

Stayed here, at the window, composing.
I was trying to compose myself

Went out later to market.
Cowheel, innards in a tub

Were such soft plethora
Near the bookshop named Arcady.

But here at my early morning perch
Watching the jay flap from branch to branch

I actually do not know
Whether I'm inside or outside.

This to be a poet is quite absurd
Where I live, in the thick of my problem.

…

Print-bound lives, that hover
In a grey mist over coarse paper

Who had a life, was found
Several books later,

The sunk island
Of metaphor gaunt with flags.

'It is corrupt of us to rhyme
Being something not in nature


To coax life out of the ground
Into museums of stillness'
He said. 'I should love lack
And welcome home its face'.

...

Now I'll go in and see her
And how her canvas is now.
It bears the weight of afternoon.

The house appeared to be empty
A you-were-there reflected silence.
Caught breath of a cold day
Tastes a thick wine,
The perfumed sediment.

Hiding inside I'll hear myself arriving
Trying out the missing voices.

6

Evening's spring sunshine, drink it down
Stand on the station platform
Smear of new green over brickwork.
The clocks have changed. I lie
On my back on the couch
And this breathing is by my left ear,
A voice in a voice
Together tracing the words:
'To be alone with the alone   and you'.

…

A certain blankness   tells me something ended
The winter sunlight   burnishing the trees
Page like a tombstone   somewhere it waits for words
This blankness  all the same   is something strange
Pentameter beat   light-ruffled leaves
Nostalgia for the unlived life
They foisted on me   shake them free
Not leaving now   until the curtain rises.

…

There is a line that left me here
As if somewhere I'd had a reader
And what became of it –
A quote from nowhere?

It is the accumulation of desires
Like pebbles in the throat
And somehow the dying
It turned back into living
Or else it turned into art.

…

The afternoon is here
A quarter to three is all it is

Leaving to go nowhere.
A poem is referred pain.

Rooted there
A plant springs up, strong writhe of stem
A musky odour to the broken leaf,

Tight blossom, a sexual sensation
As bud loosens into flower

In a small forest someone's playing.

No tenderness without anger
Yes partner me in this
As if you pricked me out
And drew me in.
Quick is our hurt
And words to cover the place.

Sweet leaves shade folly.


*A Footnote*

Mother a crazed mirror
An infant, bewildered by light
Is a wide-eyed snatching at self.

This snatched-at   it talks back at you
With its only half an idea
And later you may become
Invisible to yourself
As you disappear into those branches

Where the sunlight goes,
Into the dying leaves' stir
Their painful glory.
                        That day
Not walking to get somewhere
I reached the bridge that crosses the canal.
Plane tree leaves, afloat on the black water
Were almost perfectly still.

## A BLESSING

*Without the mortar of silence*
*The sentences crumble.*
          Hans Cohn

And this mirror?
I will murder its glass.
A reflection – like a petrified blessing
It fell out into my hand.
Here it is
The part of me that waits to be alone.

…

This child
Whose grief was a piece of burnt wood
Sublimed to an ash that I
Lifted up to my mouth.
I took myself off to the library.
For the sake of what I found there
How I suffer, in my mirror blind with understanding.

And this work? I made it myself, a mountain
That only I could climb.
Leaving behind me the valley full of home.
I will take you out of that silent home
To somewhere in the distance
Its gathering of views.

…

Disembodied
What can the head tell us?
I mean just how
Wordless can an experience be.
This absence, it will swallow up everything.

The self's an alarming weight
Whose unseen presence
Is like the voids in buildings,

A poor am. It is
The relief of less

The afternoon's trenchant murmur
And the effort to hold myself upright.

...

No longer this flurry of words onto paper
A silence will slip inside me like a song,
Lying down between the leaves of a book
Perfecting sleep in its pages.

Do I want to be part of this?
Waiting for it to be over
'It is to speak of my injuries'
My text. This careful rant
Is eating up words.

...

Unite   Untie
Whose self was a loosening knot.
It tightened in your stare
When 'I' came to the rescue.


Just another I, has started writing
Uncertain which He is I.
The pronoun spaces –
Each one like a missing step,
A moment's hesitation
Or else a dog that's faithful to its name.

...

It was age, as he came towards me
Limping into the sun.
Like one forewarned

Training myself to hear
The slow approach of silence
At the heart of desire is an absence,

Pure meaning, making no sense.
It goes to waste among the falling leaves
Look up – the bird is still there.

...

Like naming a bridge just before it
Reaches the other side,
Speech acts become them.

The speech people, look, here they come.
They are falling out of themselves,
A dry sound rattling down onto paper.

Where the light begins to end
On that building in the far distance
It lifts you closer

And where the light writes itself
The purity of that final step,
A man who kept faith with the path.


*Epitaph*
His 'case', what encases him
Then an inward rush of air
Before the enchanter died.

## SIGNING OFF

Hurt into time I have been made of words
As if in memory of my feelings
Self-sick, inhabiting a grievance.

The spaces between the lines
Are where the grief is, stepping down
From one line to the next.

. . .

The road thinks of a journey.
I lie down on my bed
Where last night I'd dreamed
My shoes full of earth.

The small, quiet detonations falter.
Tongue cool in its mouth-haven,
The solar plexus bends with love
Near enough the lips to state the hurt.

# AT CULSWICK

*The Vicarage Hatch End Middlesex*

The coalman came   face blackened   a frightened child
Inside was the bible carrier.  Census of memories,
How certain are you of almost anything?
What today lights on – a house
Now fallen into the air

The blast walls of Eden
Shrapnel souvenirs   the blackout laid aside.
Gas mask snout   old ration books
A war that you emerged from – a puzzled child
Who wondered, was this how I came?

Three generations of the men in black,
A child held up as if he were an offering.
Someone's still in there bemused by fatherhood
Playing with scripture. In the Lady Chapel
A light burned all the time, its soft blood glow.

Remote preachings of sunlight –
That was the distance I was in.
I can hardly find a way in there
To something I needed still to find,
Like a cracked jug on a shelf.

By placing it in a sort of woven basket
To carry away from there
I'd avoid its imploring gaze?
What there is of mine left, the writing.
Tracing, it to the place where I was found –

'Is it for the mother? someone asked,
That silent other who was always there.

The words were what I'd bought my silence with.
In thrall to a pair of shadows
Its nowhere has to be given a name.


*How Much More*

How much more
Of this can there be,
Family swarm
At the pierhead?

Before you arrive
You'd better forget
How it was that you came here, delivered
In a sewn up pocket.

Sad with all that weight
Being human the creature sets out
A day and a night had passed
When daylight betrayed my absence.

Walking away from the mirror
Back and forth between desk, window and bed
In a state of perpetual bafflement
It was the language stranger came to greet me.
Friendly acids came to my aid,
The language burst like a bubble inside me.
Before I forget I should like to give you this
In its sewn up pocket.

## At Culswick, Shetland

*A cage went in search of a bird*
            Kafka: *Maxims*

For your ears only? Too much to write down,
The language to soothe my throat,
It's a semi-portentous all-enclosing sound.
Trying to write itself into silence
It's a veiled game, the feigned knot of a story.

Out walking, the cliff edge feels less steady
The sea one step away. Imagine
Falling – a blaze of sun on the water
As a mouth stops shaping its noise
And the light pours out of a wound.

Lying across the beach back there
Was the dead pilot whale, pointlessly stirred
By the tide slurring the sand. Below me now
A seabird's purposeful flight just above water,
Grid pattern of cages at rest on the surface.

A boat putters out to them, it's odd
This noiseless underwater farming.
'Fish die without compunction' someone said
While a cloud halts in front of the sun.
A ragged edge of light round its edge –

Vestiges and scraps, what's left for us.
'If you wait long enough the page will refresh.'
The language still waits to be fed,
A suppressed voice, like something hurled at a window
As if to shelter a blessing.

I carried on up the track.
A curlew was defending its territory.

Perching on fence-posts or running ahead up the road
It made its quick, cheeping, warning noise.
To my left was the ruined village

A standing stone, built into a house's end wall
As if both supporting and leaving it
Everywhere stones seem perched in the wind.
We reach the broch, just below it
The place where they quarried the stone, a time-cancelling
                                            moment.

It was later that same afternoon after sleeping
I went out without a thought in my head
Into the brusque sunlight. It was only
Each particular twist in the road that was
Exercising my mind as I walked along.

The hill's side was all a complaint of sheep.
The emptied out valley, where only a few still live
Lay open like the palm of my hand
'I think that perhaps you do not quite understand,
It is not a half-hearted quest' I'd wanted to say.

But I was starting to feel at home
Among these almost abandoned fields.
I passed a slope of meadow, mixed species
Just mown, those names drying out in the sun
But not yet the pallor of art.

And now I was moving into a stiffening wind.
At the head of the valley a gate stood open.
Feeling owned by all that space
I carried on up the hill past a loch with a
Slight sense of transgression.

More and more of the bare hills ahead
Came into view, and I imagined
A child hiding out on the hillside
Reading something in a small book
Saying '*This* is where I discovered an appetite'.

Go 'looking for your voice' they'd said.
Still there was that special kind of hurt –
That square Victorian print and once again
I was trapped in its darkness.
If only I could find that book again

Swooping inward to where a child was found
Who had once sought wholesale forgiveness.
Turning home, the field-walls I passed dark with meaning
It was this I was trying to remember –
The part of me that waits to be alone.

# Three

# INSIDE THE PANOPTICON

# CENTRE AND RETREAT

With the extended family, gathered for Christmas in a rented house in Sussex. The day after our arrival we go into the town to get some provisions. There are crowds of people out shopping, lots of delicatessens and other high-end food shops. It's a strangely homogenous population, and looming over them all, on its hilltop, broods the Castle. One imagines all these people milling about down here to be a captive population kept on a sort of reservation and kept pacified with plenty of different sorts of cheese.

Back at the house. The building, Tudor with later accretions and all on different levels, is a puzzle of brick and flint. Poking out from plastered walls beams that have split are bolted and propped. The wood has turned to something like iron.

A stuffed owl inside a glass case. Temptation of locked cupboards. . . . . . Note contents of the drawer in a nondescript table on the upstairs landing: one Allen key, one Stella Artois label, one phone plug, a clothes peg, some paper clips, a table tennis net and clamps, and one book: 'The Celestine Prophecy'. In addition, and related presumably to this book, there are fliers advertising the house as a Retreat. Elsewhere in the house there are references to a Massage and Wellbeing facility in Hove under the same management.

The owner, who lives nearby, is a half-benevolent, half-threatening presence. The Visitors' Book appears to have been censored, with a half-page roughly torn out presumably because it contained unacceptable comments. The kitchen is filled with puzzling equipment and high up on a shelf there's a notice that reads *Nothing On This Shelf Works*.

The notices are everywhere: *This beautiful house is quite unique and is very much loved by its owners please look after it, respect it and enjoy it during your stay! Many thanks.* And *Due to its antiquity this loo works rather slowly! The cistern takes time to refill between flushes so you need to allow at least 3-4 minutes between pulls! There are bins provided for everything else!* Note strategic deployment of the exclamation mark, half command, half semi-humorous entreaty.

*Sorry this bidet is bust! Please do not attempt to use it.*


A walk, across chartered fields
*Emprise Security*
Delights of Sussex mist
*Euroforest*
No unauthorised person beyond this point.

This bleak burden of authority,
It settles across the shoulders
Like a stress headache.

Back in the ruined garden
In late afternoon sunlight
And the careful emprise of moss
Is it the last of England? This decline –
It's been going on for so long.

An idea still reached for
It comes back all the time
As if it never really left you
And now it arrives like a piece
Of slow and half-successful music.

Back in the house
'A couple of million to spend on it' someone sighs.
Converted to a 'Centre and Retreat'
The shelves groan with self-help books.
Your life, did it have an idea
To be signed for on departure?

We've just had a message:
'The owner's in A&E,
Heart flutter, irregular rhythms.
They might shock her tonight'.
The owner just about holding on,
Tentative yet persistent.

## THE CITIZEN UNHARMED

Look, here they come
Blowing on their quaint instruments
With major new initiatives –
The Department of Wishful Thinking.

A respectable citizen need not fear
Taking a stroll through history
And that dog? It's not the owner's fault.
This freedom is everything he pays for.

Nursing an ache, at rest in the arms of authority
It's something that reaches all the way down
Automatic as the cashpoint's greeting
Where, grinning with numbers, it levels its emptying stare.

Back home behind the houses
These stately Victorian trees. He's lost in the quiet
Brushing up on his intentions –
And that invisible part of him, how it aches!

## INSIDE THE PANOPTICON

*Establish a society in which the individual*
*Has to pay for the air he breathes*
*(Air meters, imprisonment*
*And rarefied air in case of non-payment)*
*Asphyxiation, if need be*
*Cut off the air*
          Marcel Duchamp

Its text box-fresh
Where happiness is a serious business.
But O the melancholia of being a camera –
Looking all round you might make you disappear.


Sunday and hurried on by sunlight
Through the City, almost empty
Past unfrequented churches
The money seems asleep
So many windows you are mirrored in
Black glass, it's a district of shades
And this one visiting stranger.


They collect here in spaces hollowed out by money
As if they are in awe of themselves.

'I was in sight of a death' one said
'And how this thing took hold of me

Look at me here
And gaze on my misfortune'.

Reflections of buildings taking flight into buildings
That briefly interrupt sun's headstrong glare

But the power out of these soft faces…
And the way having money, it makes you feel chosen.


Here a handful of trees have been planted, in careful containers
To declare what remains of the seasons.
A financial system?
It's like an abandoned playground.
Its machinery of forgetting
Is blind as a temple façade.

There are puzzling arenas
And people kept hanging about.
Where the future devours itself
They wait to become a statistic.


*Payback*

'You will pay for what I did to you'.
In here the poor will defeat the poor
'Tell me, how do you find our language?'
For lack of a paradise these fell back.
Their dignity like a suit of clothes
Hidden away in a cupboard
They defend themselves against charity
With only a handful of words.
Halted on giant screens
There are faces stupid with significance
And production of more titles:
'Breathing For Tomorrow –
How to Save More Air'.

*A Gallerist Speaks*

Sunrise onto particulars –
Through a skylight
A passing cloud watches.
Art shavings are being curated
Lapsed cloth-sign in a corner.
A gallery's trapped air –
Significant art moments
Are looking in at themselves.
What else was there, in the absence of a cure?


*Lip Service*

Sung through pursed lips
A scream at the ready, the planned
Metamorphosis of your stare,
Animals taken home in bags
Their blood streams out past you.

Elasticity is the holding together
Of all the conventions of pain. Lips move
Soundlessly where I tread.
This fissure – the street
Is injury and its image.
Over the pavements go the unformed millions.

 An odd happiness
Slides in under the door
Where I've come to rest, in a
Room full of mirrors

*Train Journey*

'Reporting anything unusual won't hurt you'

You have to have it – it's there
And comfortable to lean on
Blending into the same sign
That tells you where the people are –
Hidden somewhere behind that billboard.
But I am just passing through
Spectating the spectacle.
Being forbidden the outside air
It's hard to say what I'm near.
I might write it down on my hand.
As I lean into my journey
I feel I am being edged out
Of somewhere I never quite was
Passing these large bare fields,
Here and there coverts, concealing birds
Carefully reared for the gun.

# SOME NOTES ON COINAGE

*Prelude*

Early October, afternoon's
Gold light   how soft is the air.
She's working in the garden.

The water boatmen
Are skating over the pond,
Apparently random movements –
You can't see where they touch
The water's surface
And it makes me think of numbers on a screen.

At the back of the house, we two
Mortgage redeemed, dead pledge. Indoors
An anxious collector resides
Turning over his coins
In a dusty afternoon light.


*The Collector*

Coin-collecting: the province of the autodidact? In a basement in Bloomsbury a dozen or so middle-aged men are gathered for a meeting of the Numismatic Club. Carausius, the 'British' emperor who became a subject of particular interest in the late 18th Century, is the speaker's topic. He suggests the two medallions of Carausius in the British Museum may be 18th Century forgeries.

Given up by the ground to the air,
A crop of metal. It's as if
The earth were to give up its dead.
The past's a cold touch of metal.

Tonight it's the matter of Britain –
And there's even a 'British' emperor.
His coin I bought, scarcely more
Than a blemish in the ground

It was 'Found on the A5 near Wendover:
Semi-barbarous radiate featuring pax'.
It's a real dog of a coin

But these two medallions found in the hush of a drawer –
In the eighteenth century, 'fine old cabinet tone'.
Were they forging an empire?

Somewhere I have that coin of Caesar,
Silver denarius, scorched father,
City – its palladium rescued
To start it all over again.

And as for you
Do you want to collect every emperor?
Maybe now is the time to compose
An elegy for coinage
Today there are simply these screens –
But still there's this ringing
Down at the roots of my teeth: I must have metal!

*Carausius AE antoninus, Rev. Pax Aug. Struck in Colchester in 292/293?*
*Julius Caesar AR Denarius. Issue of 47-46 BC. Diademed head of Venus. Reverse: Aeneas advancing left holding Palladium and carrying Anchises on left shoulder. "Caesar" on reverse.*

*The Silver Mines at Laurion*

*And again there is land that has silver beneath it, clearly by divine allotment: for though many cities are our neighbours, both by land and sea, not even a single small vein of silver ore goes through into any of them.*
                    Xenophon

Few visit the place, it is said.
The watchtowers have fallen
And finished all that turmoil under the ground.
They were perhaps ten thousand
Slaves at work in the mines.

It sits in the palm of your hand
'From the author's collection'
This silver thing.
It has an antique glare,

*Silver tetradrachm circa 440 BC. Head of Athena. Reverse: owl standing r.*


*Lyttos*

'Coins of crude style'
Soft slug of metal, and then
Where the punch took aim
The moment of impact's preserved
And the strike, its time-cancelling quality
Where the boar's head surfaced from metal
And an eagle, in blurred flight.

*Silver stater, Crete: 320-270 BC Eagle flying l. Reverse: boar's head in dotted square contained within incuse square. The eagle: Diktaian Zeus, the boar: Artemis*

*Syracuse*

Zeus *eleutherios*
'Bringer of political freedom'
Time of Timoleon,
The one who was sent for from Corinth.
Zeus: right father,
The big-chinned man
Trapped in the blunt metal,
Lightning bolt on the reverse
And next to it a small eagle.

Syracuse – you remember
Where we stayed in that odd hotel,
It was full of puzzling empty rooms

And outside a harbour. All day
The owner stood at the desk and stared out to sea
But the ships had all sailed away.

Six am and I've found another on ebay
'Granular patina'. Seated in front of the screen
I am wondering
Is this the freedom we sent for –
Does it come from the sky, in a
Bundle of lightnings,
Such lavish expedition?
Day breaks, still here
I plead my cause to the sky.

*AE hemilitron, Sicily, Syracuse 334-336BC. Head of Zeus Eleutherios. Reverse: Thunderbolt; eagle standing r. in field to r.*

Four

AN INTERZONE

## THE DIARIST

The diarist's a
Transcendental body engineered
And the zone? It is here
In a cluttered book,
Objects relating / reacting poetically
When like a child remembering to play
I opened it once again
Chipping away at the silence.
And how is *your* burden –
Being looked back at
Still in the shadow of that language
From which the mortal odours rise.

## POSE

*I am hoping to make a new thing for the world that remains in the mind like a new species of living thing*
                    Frank Auerbach

But maybe the words were a holding off
From something quite simple
And it's hard to say what I'm near.
That silent partner the body
Is crossing the studio floor
Treading a pattern of sunlight falling in
From the window behind
To where the artist has lifted his brush.
He is holding it just there
In front of the canvas. His is the actual pose.
He is drawing a line round a shadow
Not certain what's coming alive –
Is it nature caught in the act? He remembers
That light and shadow never stay still.
The echo I am still follows
But before he can hand it over
To ownership of the eyes
Restless as ever
He has organised his escape from the picture.

## LATE

October, the year's late sunlight
Is stalking the ground.
Slanting through branches
How far the light reaches in
And the trees, their stilted performance.

A sense of baffled expectation,
Is this what weighs the branches down?
It almost reaches to where you are
An infant again,
The puzzle of itself being awake,

An echo being the sound you make
Finding yourself over here
In the realm of the almost forgotten.

Draining the pool of its silence.
On a day of triumphant stillness
Enough is almost too much, and now these
Late-flowering peaceful torments?

Still learning to be here,
This 'you'. It is a silence inside me
Caught in its bubble of breath.

## STONE BOAT

It was built to the shape of a person
Who stands near, alive and well
Is a life we've scarcely lived
I declare, still paying lip-service
To the child hiding its breath in a paper boat.

Always the invisible family
Tracks the dead light in our footsteps,
Handprint burnt into a mirror, or as bright
As a photograph, its insistent values
Where each of them's named to such stillness.

Coffin, stone boat inside here
Held over against traffic.
What stretches itself out
Is heavy, dark and almost blind,
                                    Imagined
A flutter of stone lids.

## HIS NIGHT THOUGHTS

Sleep crossing the barricades
The words are a sleeping army
Held over against morning.

Another 'significant pause'
An assault on the breath
And these poems are merely
The words seeking forgiveness?

The four-year-olds, playing out in the garden,
They've made an imaginary insect trap.
What if these finished poems were all just drafts,
Will that be enough to hide me in the hereafter?

...

The part of me that lives to be alone
It looks down at the water
From its shelf of sky. That sea,
It is a nothing to be with
A thronging mirror
That encroached on our beginnings.

Reading you halfway through the afternoon.
We are together in the afternoon
When in a sudden lurch to friendship
You are beside me like a welcome absence.

So, mastering the silence
I'll finish my reply to you –
Enjoy what's in your mouth
Else it perish.

...

Sleeping, waking to read then sleeping again.
February's whitish light's
The nothing of an afternoon,
People exchanging poems for all they're worth
To simplify each state of mind
And manage pain.

So while you're about it
What is it you are about?
Called 'Give Me Back My Past'

The idol-maker, grieving for himself
'Your job is to keep me alive'
He has come here dressed like a wound –

'Look at my wound
I am all wound
Come here, admire my wound'

. . .

Bright winter sky   some cirrus.
My own blood, ours

Making the most of what there is
Being lofty, is almost as high.
Imitate transcendence
Like catching an echo.

And if I were to come back
As someone like you
A body recovering appetite
Warbling –

It's about not owning
This temporary perch

Just holding on in the wind
To steadily wavering energies.

# THE PARADISE FILE

*They caress the indignant river*
           Kafka, *Maxims*

These others are victims as well.
Out there on the opposing bank
You can hear their language, like prancing on stilts,
The discussants' ridiculous laughter.

As if someone were to lie down
At the threshold of himself
Still trying to understand
That this was his share of the world.

What they have become
In spite of themselves,
Is these voices, slaves of the wind.

. . .

The fruit – it hangs down?
Well yes, it depends

The good life being what he most feared
With its echo of paradise.

'Come closer to me and I'll tell you
It is a mistake we are here.'

She turned round and smiled and he was
Ash in her gaze.

'It was this awakening undid me
When I fell out into the sky.

Unspeakable it came to meet my lips.
I suffered lyric harm.'

. . .

An epitaph is what marks the place
Where a man fell into
A book like a floating bird hide.
His death – exemplary for once
He's a perfect fit in his frame.

Like public art it is
Being hidden in the open air
When a window opens and closes all at once
And the room is a perfect absence,
Light sitting in the chair.

. . .

I came out here in hope of little
So these be my words
Brought with me, my
Nostalgia for the unlived life
I am so thick with it
Showing you things my way to being
Intimate. And here are my
Silences you can have
If you so like it.

Myself, I was conceived
In hope say what I like of it
With all my angry mutter. Now
A voice outside is singing to itself
As if to bargain for an echo
Somewhere behind the page.

It hurries to the blood
Forcing the thing to grow
And welcome so much damage.
'This is a hard thing'
The child thought, braving a lonely paradise
Hoping that tall and vaulting shadow
Might simply take him home from harm.

## TAKEN FLIGHT

The Summer is ending and the swifts have almost all gone, no longer charging in squadrons above our garden. All that is left is the occasional speck in the sky which make me think of particles of dust trapped under a picture's glass.

Out walking that time in Dorset
We'd reached the top of the slope
And there they were, the gliders
Nestling against the side of the hill.

Now the first swift I've seen this year
Is scything the air with its moments
And bird man's a sort of pause
As if it were his way,
This flying, of hiding up there
And maybe about to
Abandon his sky refuge.

...

Library, and the ache of sunlight
Coming in to find me.

Comforts of existence;
The cold comfort of words.

It came from further off, like an echo
Whose noise went distant in the afternoon.

A place where everything is absorbed
Was what I'd ached to find.

What I liked was an Autumn ruination of gardens – yes
As if I were leaning over an afterwards.

Carved with names the stone founds a silence.
Where do I speak from now?

'Give me the world of art and its comfortable distances'
I made a world and I peopled it with myself

A sort of warm smell,
Yet I was in such an anxiety of waiting.

. . .

The dying fall has died again
Busy odes
Lyric sailing like a tidy boat.

Which is where I might begin, in lonely delight
The accident of substance, words that seem to arrive
From a significant distance.

You two who released me
Into becoming,
You two who are air

Voices from mouths with broken teeth
Making mouth music.
How can you sing to an empty mouth?

Outside the leaves are changing into time,
A blurred gaze of statuary. Here
It was simply the oddness of being in a voice.

*Coda*

Lawn is a skin
Of cold, wetness, this
Living
      Dawn, lips and a
New wind blows
Across old fields
Frozen with star light,
Room for a change.
What was ours not being ours
But this wind is friendly,
It is not to know where it
Blows from, it brings
Its smell of damp leaves.
A new cock crows
In the old star light
Opens the dawn
A paleness bleeds in
And the new life brings
What we inherit
Out into the change.
Waking to write
The paper grown pale beside me
Moving, small and unseen, out into
The chill air's greeting
And all the old life
Swings round, the forgotten
Facing the new,
Here is the old world
Speaking to the new.

## SQUANDERED GLANCES

Statue, brought back
Each stranger limb
And a drop of forgotten blood.

Gate of pink granite.

The taste of that expulsion
Because someone died? An itch in the silence,
That was the language they had brought me to
A gloomy temple to an unknown god.

An unwritten poem
Breathed *thou* at my side
Incredulous   feel that wound.

It makes a life   here where
My head is in my hands
Watching the words cross the page
In a rush toward silence.

Well, these are my hands
As I breathe out my breath.

. . .

The rain the rain.
The garden waved goodbye.
What I was listening out for
That half-heard music, was a sort of greeting.
It fades with the meaning of words
As the quick self flies away into time

Looking up at the apples
Where they ripen against the blue,

Holding the syllable under my tongue.
It was abstract but delicious. Next day
I walked out over a lawn wet with dew,
Green apples hunched in the grass.

Leaving the train
And coming out onto the street
The rain had stopped, and now the sun – this moment
A cheerful abyss of self.
The evening is cool and clear.

# NOTES

*Carpenter build me a house* (p.9)
Zimmer, a carpenter, in a letter to the poet Hölderlin's mother. Hölderlin spent the last thirty-six years of his life, after he had been declared insane, living with Zimmer and his family.

*Not At All* (p.23)
Sources and references include among others Thomas Heywood, T.S. Eliot's essays, Malevich etc.

*At Ranters Lodge* (p.29-33)
Ranters Lodge on the Isle of Portland in Dorset was formerly a Methodist chapel, and opposite stands a building formerly used as a mortuary and known as The Dead House. Conjuror's Lodge, nearby, was another Methodist chapel set up in the early nineteenth century by a breakaway group who refused to renounce a belief in witchcraft. Southwell is a village on Portland. The Isle of Portland has two prisons and various former military installations.

*After du Bellay* (p.58-59)
This is a version of Sonnet XII 'Je vy sourdre d'un roc un vive fontaine' from the 16th century French poet Joachim du Bellay's 'Les Antiquitez de Rome'.

*A Blessing* (p.66)
Hans Cohn was a psychotherapist who wrote in German and practised in the UK. His poems were published by Menard Press, in a translation by his brother.

*Whose grief was a piece of burnt wood* (p.66)
Sent away to boarding school aged nine I complained to the school matron of constant stomach aches and was given charcoal tablets as a remedy for indigestion.

*Pose* (p.120)
The exhibition 'Silent Partners' was held at the Fitzwilliam Museum, Cambridge in 2014. This poem refers to a painting in the exhibition by Alan Beeton.

www.ingramcontent.com/pod-product-compliance
Lightning Source LLC
Chambersburg PA
CBHW031158160426
43193CB00008B/423